SUCCESS ACCELERATION & MASTERY

7 SUCCESS KEYS TO A PROFOUNDLY MEANINGFUL AND & PURPOSEFUL LIFE

Table of Contents

Why another course on success? 1

My story 2

Meet Mitch 3

My Own Massive Transformation 4

What we're going to learn in this course 5

What does success mean to you? 6

Successful People don't necessarily define success with fame & fortune 7

Stephen Covey 8

Drugs in Ancient Cultures: A History of Drug Use and Effects 9

Warren Buffett 10

Maya Angelou 11

Oprah Winfrey 12

Deepak Chopra 13

Some of your favorite C.E.O.'s 14

So, what are these people telling us about their success? 15

Why are we lied to 16

What are the keys to a successful & happy life? 17

How should we redefine success? 18

We don't do success alone or just for our benefit 19

How to Live a More Meaningful Life 20

Pointers on creating meaning 21

Prioritize Connection With Others 22

Do For Others 23

Express Yourself 24

Courage is Key..25

Meaning and Happiness Aren't Always Interlinked.........................26

A deeper, more meaningful life will follow..27

Life is a whole different experience when you understand what guides you...28

The Missing Piece to the Purpose Puzzle 29

Finding Yourself=..30

The Actual, Practical Part of Living on Purpose................................31

What are the 7 principles?..32

Stop living in a conditional, contingent world of "If-Then..."............33

How to be happy?..34

What does it mean to be charitable & Help others?.........................35

How do you accelerate your success?..36

KEY TAKE-AWAYS FROM THIS COURSE 37

Next steps on your healing journey..38

WHY ANOTHER COURSE ON SUCCESS?

- Because we have it all backwards! In order to be successful, you're supposed to be happy, too
- But, all the evidence shows that Happiness must precede Success to work
- Wisdom shows that "Success" is not about external things like money, fame, and fortune, things
- Rather, Success means that we have found our true purpose in life, find meaning doing it, and can succeed because we are focusing on our "WHY"?
- What? We are learning all the wrong stuff as kids, in college and grad school. It's not having the big house and nice car, or acquiring lots of things. It's not about having a big title and salary
- It's about finding your true purpose in life and living it to the best of your ability
- We are setting ourselves and our kids up for dismal failure and unhappiness and a life not well lived if we don't drastically rethink this "Success" thing!

MY STORY

 I was taught to make a lot of money and have a lot of things = those silly old-school Europeans!

 I was taught that I needed to be competitive, aggressive, and climb my way to the top the ladder

 I was taught that I needed to take risk if I wanted to succeed

 I did all those things, became "successful" - had all the trappings of a "successful" life

 I was never taught a thing about seeking happiness – that was just falsely assumed that this would happen after success

 I ended up being miserable, stressed out, overwhelmed, and incredibly unhappy until I let go of all those false assumptions and focused on happiness first

MEET MITCH

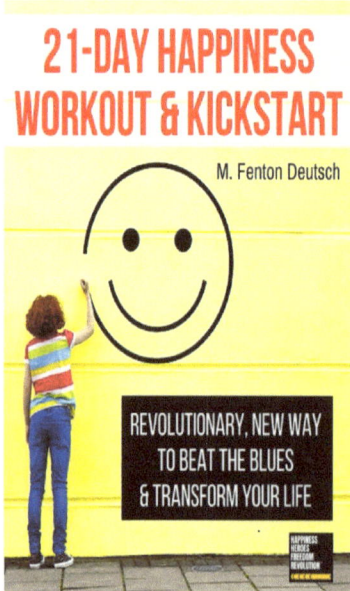
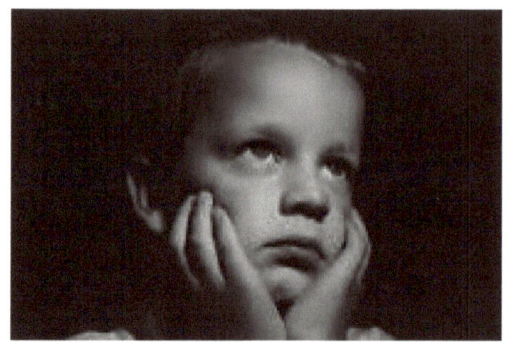

MY OWN MASSIVE TRANSFORMATION
I decided to heal everything!

Mitch Before @ Age 55

- 310 lbs.
- *On 15 Medications
- Walking with a cane
- Workaholic
- Addicted to Alcohol & Pills
- Kids & ex-wife hate me
- Few Friends
- Angry & Burnt Out
- Lonely, Irritable, Discontent
- Couch Potato
- Very Sad & Mad

Mitch After @ Age 62

- 199 lbs.
- *Medication Free
- *Workout 5 days/week – totally buff
- Doing what I love with total balance
- Substance Free
- Healed relationships with Family & Friends
- Deep & Loving Friendships at home and at work.
- Free from my past and living in the incredible flow and gifts of my life.
- Meditate & do Yoga, Spin & Cross Fit
- Happy, fulfilled & smiling, relaxed & truly grateful to be alive! At peace with my life & the universe

WHAT WE'RE GOING TO LEARN IN THIS COURSE

- What true success is and how to accelerate and master it
- Why happiness must be your priority if you're going to be truly successful
- How you can have it all – if you master your happiness blueprint first
- How to develop meaning and find your purpose in life
- The 7 success keys to keep you both happy and successful!

WHAT DOES SUCCESS MEAN TO YOU?

- According to Merriam-Webster's definition of "success," anyone who's rich, respected, or famous is successful. ... I like this definition way better — it still encompasses the above description (your personal goals can include making lots of money!), but also includes people who think more outside of the box:

- 1. Achievement of an action within a specified period of time or within a specified parameter. Success can also mean completing an objective or reaching a goal. Success can be expanded to encompass an entire project or be restricted to a single component of a project or task. It can be achieved within the workplace, or in an individual's personal life. For example, if an individual's personal goal is to be accepted in a new career, success would occur after the individual has been officially accepted into his or her new place of employment. 2. Colloquial term used to describe a person that has achieved his or her personal, financial or career goals. It could also be used to describe an individual that has more objects (money or any other desirable item) relative to another individual. For example, a professional athlete can be called "a success." Read more: http://www.businessdictionary.com/definition/success.html

SUCCESSFUL PEOPLE DON'T NECESSARILY DEFINE SUCCESS WITH FAME & FORTUNE

 Well, for one, they already have it, so it's easy to say so after the fact

 Successful people don't necessarily define success as being rich or powerful.

 Instead, they often talk about relationships, well-being, and societal impact.

 I think it's really ok to be professionally and materially successful, but you have to make sure you are putting in all the sweat and tears for the right thing for you and that it resonates with who you are – which is more than just an accumulation of things and titles!!

STEPHEN COVEY

- Stephen Covey dedicated his life to discovering the idea of success and traits that make someone effective. The Harvard educated author, educator, businessman, and keynote speaker launched into the mainstream with his book "The 7 Habits of Highly Effective People." Overnight, Covey became one of the most successful authors in the world.

- His book stayed on the New York Times bestseller list for an unprecedented 250 weeks and sold over 25 million copies. You might think Covey would give his readers and listeners a clear idea of what success looked like to him, but this is not the case. Covey told the New York Times he believed success was categorically individual:

- "If you carefully consider what you want to be said of you in the funeral experience you will find your definition of success."

DRUGS IN ANCIENT CULTURES: A HISTORY OF DRUG USE AND EFFECTS

Arianna Huffington has appeared on Forbes' most powerful women list, is a New York Times best-selling author, and one of the most successful media moguls of all time. In 1974, she published her first book and in 1980 moved from London to the United States.

In the early 2000s, she ran for Governor of California and in 2005 launched the award-winning news platform in Huffington Post. Huffington says that even though we tend to think of success along the two lines- money and power- we need to add a third:

"To live the lives we truly want and deserve, and not just the lives we settle for, we need a Third Metric a third measure of success that goes beyond the two metrics of money and power, and consists of four pillars: well-being, wisdom, wonder, and giving."

WARREN BUFFETT

- Warren Buffett is one of the most well-known and respected businessmen in the entire world. From an early age, Buffet created and sold businesses. He was even able to put himself through college with the profits made from one of his childhood companies. The "Oracle of Omaha" became a lifelong student, learning from each and every opportunity that he was presented with.

- Over the course of his life, Buffett's business ventures would go into everything from media, insurance, energy, and the food industry. The celebrated philanthropist net worth would eventually grow to over $84 billion. In 2006, Buffet announced he would be giving away his entire fortune to charity, most of it going to Bill Gates' foundation. Same for Buffet, the definition of success isn't money or fame:

- "I measure success by how many people love me."

MAYA ANGELOU

- Maya Angelou was an accomplished author, poet laureate, songwriter, director, and civil rights, activist. She was best known for seven autobiographical books, one of which was nominated for the National Book Award. Angelou's career was full of groundbreaking moments including being the first African American women director in Hollywood.
- Throughout the end of the 1950s Angelou worked closely with Dr. Martin Luther King on the Civil Right Movement. At the request of Bill Clinton, Angelou delivered her poem "On the Pulse of the Morning" at his 1993 inauguration. Then in 2010, President Obama awarded Angelou the Presidential Medal of Freedom. Angelou's success wasn't defined by being groundbreaking or her award recognition, success is all about liking what you do:
- "Success is liking yourself, liking what you do, and liking how you do it."

OPRAH WINFREY

- Oprah Winfrey came from humble and rough beginnings. She was able to turn her life around in her teenage years and focused on a television career. Winfrey worked for local Baltimore stations, but faced setbacks and discrimination. When she finally had the chance to have her own show, she continually came last in ratings.

- But Oprah never gave up and switched the formatting of her show. Her relatability skyrocketed her to becoming America's First Lady of talk shows. After the success of her show, Oprah started a magazine, a production company, and multiple charitable organizations. However, for Oprah success isn't being known by just her first name or being one of the world's wealthiest women, success to her is all about feeling fulfilled:

- "…How to be used in the greater service to life. Ask this question, and the answer will be returned and rewarded to you with fulfillment, which is the major definition of success, to me."

DEEPAK CHOPRA

 Spiritual teacher Deepak Chopra believes success is a matter of constant growth.

 The physician and author says it's a matter of continual growth.

 "Success in life could be defined as the continued expansion of happiness and the progressive realization of worthy goals," Chopra writes in "The Seven Spiritual Laws of Success."

SOME OF YOUR FAVORITE C.E.O.'S...

- "To find and fully live your purpose in life; and to leave an enduring legacy of having made a difference in the world."
- -- Ron Cordes, founder of the Cordes Foundation
- "Success is not having to describe what's been accomplished.....others do it for you"
- -- Deborah Hopkins, Chief Innovation Officer of Citibank
- "I define success as living my true purpose and having a positive impact on the lives of people by uplifting them and inspiring them to think and act in ways that they may not have considered before."
- -- Raj Sisodia, co-founder of Conscious Capitalism and professor at Babson College
- "The purpose of our lives is to contribute our unique, God-given gifts to have an extraordinary positive impact on the lives of others and the world."
- -- David Kidder, CEO of Bionic
- "Success, for me, has always been in providing a great quality of life for my family, for those who work for me, and to my community."
- -- Jeremy Young CEO of Tanga

SO, WHAT ARE THESE PEOPLE TELLING US ABOUT THEIR SUCCESS?

- It's not only about power, money, fame, being #1
- It usually includes some benefits to other people
- It isn't done alone – "it takes a village"
- It includes "Living Your Purpose" (which assumes you understand what it is)
- Most people say that it must make a difference in the world or leave a legacy
- It should include constant growth and happiness??
- It should include being of greater service to "life"
- I like Maya Angelou's the best: "Success is liking yourself, liking what you do, and liking how you do it."

WHY ARE WE LIED TO

- So, why all this bravado and hype growing up about getting the best grades, overscheduling our lives to take a million activities as kids, beating the competition, fancy cars, lots of dough, big houses in the best burbs or up high in the sky?

- We are pummeled in school, by the media, social media, by our families, by society about being the best and brightest. Second best isn't good enough.

- At what cost to our sanity and well-being are we willing to go to be really materially successful

- How much power, fame, and fortune do we really need?

- When is enough really enough (quick story, my successful friends and I talked about whether we needed $5mm, $20mm, or $50mm to retire. I was 25 full of spit and fire, and always felt that working really hard and succeeding always came first – often at the expense of my self or my family – even health)

WHAT ARE THE KEYS TO A SUCCESSFUL & HAPPY LIFE?

- We are responsible & accountable for our lives 100% - No blaming spoken here
- We MUST know and fully understand our "WHY"
- We need to know what we want and how to define our success
- We need to develop our plan, priorities, and best way to get there
- We must be hungry and motivated
- We must accept that the process is a journey, and each day counts
- We must accept adversity, challenge, & failure as the pathway to success
- We must always stay grateful, humble, honest, and learn acceptance
- We must include happiness is one of the keys in any formula for success

HOW SHOULD WE REDEFINE SUCCESS?

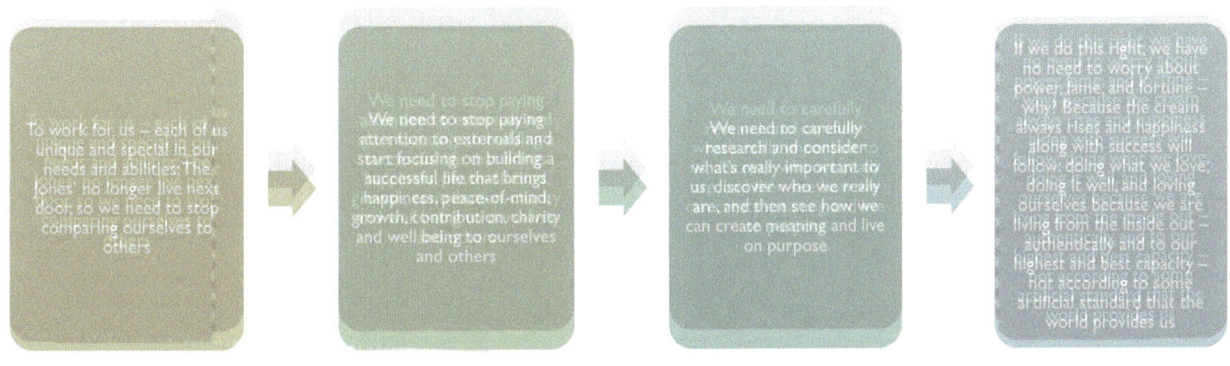

- To work for us – each of us unique and special in our needs and abilities; The Jones' no longer live next door, so we need to stop comparing ourselves to others

- We need to stop paying attention to externals and start focusing on building a successful life that brings happiness, peace-of-mind, growth, contribution, charity and well-being to ourselves and others

- We need to carefully research and consider what's really important to us, discover who we really are, and then see how we can create meaning and live on purpose

- If we do this right, we have no need to worry about power, fame, and fortune – why? Because the cream always rises and happiness along with success will follow: doing what we love, doing it well, and loving ourselves because we are living from the inside out – authentically and to our highest and best capacity – not according to some artificial standard that the world provides us

WE DON'T DO SUCCESS ALONE OR JUST FOR OUR BENEFIT

- I believe that we all have a very unique mission on this earth
- That mission is to heal our past, stop fearing the future, and start living in the present moment – where our lives are really being lived
- We need to know thyself and then be true to ourselves
- We need to establish and adopt a set of values that makes us feel good in our own skin, the we need to walk the walk from this inside strength
- We need to stop with the "I", "Me" and the self-centeredness and separateness that sadly defines our world and become an integral and active part of the world
- We need to fully engage with other people and develop good, loving and supportive relationships that matter
- We need to focus our happiness on having meaningful and great experiences in life and not on accumulating wealth and notoriety!
- Once we find out what we're best at and what we love to do, then we must do the very best we can while considering others along the way

HOW TO LIVE A MORE MEANINGFUL LIFE

- "Above all else, experiencing a meaningful life means living in the moment, while connecting the past, the present, and the future. Doing so gives us a clearer idea of where we need to go in light of where we have been.
- Satisfaction and MeaningLiving a life that has some kind of meaning is one of the most widely held goals in existence -- something by which we motivate and measure ourselves.
- Just how to do this is a conundrum that has challenged philosophers, scientists, and so many people throughout the ages.
- But perhaps the solution may not be as complex as it seems.
- While there is no single answer, research has shown that there are several factors that influence our ability to find satisfaction and meaning in life.Source: Huffpost.com ByPeter Field, ContributorPsychotherapist
- Here then are a few pointers:

POINTERS ON CREATING MEANING

- "Develop a sense of Purpose
- If there is one factor that influences our ability to live a meaningful life it's having a sense of purpose -- a reason to get out of bed in the morning and to keep on going.
- Not only does a sense of purpose fuel a sense of meaning in life, but it also brings with it more time in which to enjoy that meaning.
- Research conducted at the University of Rochester has shown that having a sense of purpose in life not only increases the quality of our lives, but may also help us to live longer -- regardless of our age. [1]
- What's more, the longevity benefits remained, even after other factors, such as relationships and positive emotions were factored in.
- The take-away message is clear: having a sense of purpose is an important component in a long and meaningfully lived life."
- Source: Huffpost.com ByPeter Field, ContributorPsychotherapist

PRIORITIZE CONNECTION WITH OTHERS

- "Joint research conducted by psychologists from Stanford University, Florida State University, and the University of Minnesota shows that connection to others is necessary in order to bring meaning to our life. [2]
- Being close to others, family or friends, results in a greater feeling of purpose, enhancing life's meaning.
- This doesn't mean that we have to live in an ideal, perfectly harmonious family or social environment. The researchers clarify that connection to others should not be mistaken for "perfect" relationships. Quite the contrary, the process of conflict with relevant others, and the time invested in overcoming challenges and disagreements, can serve to deepen those relationships, so increasing life's meaning.
- Simply having those connections -- even though stress may accompany them -- is enough to give our lives a deeper sense of meaning."
- Source: Huffpost.com ByPeter Field, ContributorPsychotherapist

DO FOR OTHERS

- "It's no great secret that giving to others improves our own feelings of purpose and meaning. Giving can take many forms, of course: donating our time, or our talents -- or simply lending a friendly ear.
- Helping others seems to be strongly correlated with increased life satisfaction. Lending a helping hand can provide a sense of purpose for us, young and old.
- One fascinating aspect of working for the benefit of others is that helping others improves both physical and mental health. In fact, studies show that involvement in community service activities is linked to living longer. [3]
- But volunteering once every now and then appears to be of little real use. If it is to have any meaningful impact, there is a threshold a person must meet when it comes to being of service to others.
- Giving our time in order to help others on a more regular basis, will bring the greatest rewards in terms of enhancing life's meaning, while maximizing our positive impact on the people with whom we come into contact.
- In short, helping and doing good for others is an important component of any meaningfully lived life -- it pays real dividends."
- Source: Huffpost.com ByPeter Field, ContributorPsychotherapist

EXPRESS YOURSELF

- "Living a meaningful life is closely related to authenticity, to being who we truly are.
- Many people struggle to be themselves for fear of criticism or rejection; as a result, they find themselves living a life that is far from satisfying or meaningful. When we are not allowed -- for whatever reason -- to be who we truly are, we greatly diminish the meaning we can derive from the life we live.
- An excellent example of this is the recent transition, or gender affirmation, of Bruce Jenner to Caitlyn Jenner. Ms. Jenner lived her life for 65 years as someone whom she felt was not aligned with her true nature. Now that her gender affirmation is complete, she is at last able to express her authentic self, and in so doing, she is more able to live a life of greater meaning.
- Here, then, is another important factor in our ability to live a meaningful life: We must be willing to live in an authentic way, one that allows us to express who we truly are -- even if this takes courage."
- Source: Huffpost.com ByPeter Field, ContributorPsychotherapist

COURAGE IS KEY

- "The simple fact is that sometimes it takes courage to live. And it can take even more courage to live a meaningful life. It can be all too easy to fall into the rut of habit, seldom reaching out, trying fresh, new things. People who lead meaningful lives put themselves out there, they try new things, challenge the way they think, and doggedly seek out that which they want from life. A good way to look at courage is to view it as a kind of tenacious willingness. An attitude of being willing to try something a little different -- perhaps even something scary -- in order to develop and maximize the meaning we derive from life. Courage means being willing to make connections with others. Being willing to help our fellow travelers on life's road. Being willing to care. As the ancient Chinese philosopher Lao Tzu put it: "From caring comes courage." When we have this kind of willingness then a deeper, more meaningful life will surely follow."
- Source: Huffpost.com ByPeter Field, ContributorPsychotherapist

MEANING AND HAPPINESS AREN'T ALWAYS INTERLINKED

- "While we can be happy and find meaning in life, the two don't always go hand in hand. [4] Living meaningfully means that we need to accept the fact that there will be bumps, bruises, and perhaps even unhappiness along the way.
- Above all else, experiencing a meaningful life means living in the moment, while connecting the past, the present, and the future. Doing so gives us a clearer idea of where we need to go in light of where we have been.
- Life itself is a process, and viewing things in their proper context -- particularly our struggles and our sadnesses -- is associated with greater meaning and a sense of purpose. [5]
- Perhaps psychiatrist and Auschwitz survivor Viktor Frankl said it best:
- "If there is meaning in life at all, then there must be meaning in suffering."
- "Life is without meaning. You bring the meaning to it." -- Joseph Campbell"
- Source: Tiny Buddha By Jacob Sokol https://tinybuddha.com/blog/what-you-need-to-live-a-life-of-purpose

A DEEPER, MORE MEANINGFUL LIFE WILL FOLLOW…

- "The simple fact is that sometimes it takes courage to live. And it can take even more courage to live a meaningful life. It can be all too easy to fall into the rut of habit, seldom reaching out, trying fresh, new things. People who lead meaningful lives put themselves out there, they try new things, challenge the way they think, and doggedly seek out that which they want from life. A good way to look at courage is to view it as a kind of tenacious willingness. An attitude of being willing to try something a little different -- perhaps even something scary -- in order to develop and maximize the meaning we derive from life. Courage means being willing to make connections with others. Being willing to help our fellow travelers on life's road. Being willing to care. As the ancient Chinese philosopher Lao Tzu put it: "From caring comes courage." When we have this kind of willingness then a deeper, more meaningful life will surely follow."
- Source: Tiny Buddha By Jacob Sokol   https://tinybuddha.com/blog/what-you-need-to-live-a-life-of-purpose

LIFE IS A WHOLE DIFFERENT EXPERIENCE WHEN YOU UNDERSTAND WHAT GUIDES YOU.

- "The Different Types of Purposes
- Fortunately for us, we're in much better situations than Frankl was, meaning we're in a different boat with finding purpose. When living a practical life of purpose, we can see the picture on both a "micro" level and a "macro" level.
- Your micro level purpose is to know your values, and then, be in integrity with them. When you know what you stand for, and do what you believe in, your confidence and sense of self-worth will be sky-high, regardless of how much the situation sucks.
- But that's only part of living on purpose.
- Your macro level purpose is something different. It's the big picture. It's your search for meaning. It's your ultimate goal. It's waking up in the morning knowing you're on the right path, regardless of what other people say.
- In his Tiny Buddha contribution, Discovering Happiness through Purpose in 3 Natural Steps, Scott Dinsmore explored three things that must align for you to discover your purpose: values, strengths, and passions. However, there's one vital piece to the purpose puzzle that's missing."
- Source: Tiny Buddha By Jacob Sokol https://tinybuddha.com/blog/what-you-need-to-live-a-life-of-purpose

THE MISSING PIECE TO THE PURPOSE PUZZLE

- "Your purpose is about giving, not getting.
- We all want to better ourselves and our lives, but purpose – like success and happiness – is counterintuitive. Here's what Viktor Frankl said about service:
- "Don't aim at success. The more you aim at it and make it a target, the more you are going to miss it. For success, like happiness, cannot be pursued; it must ensue, and it only does so as the unintended side effect of one's personal dedication to a cause greater than oneself or as the by-product of one's surrender to a person other than oneself."
- You want love from people? Love people! You want more money? Help people make money! You want more joy in life? Give joy to people! Sounds so simple, right?
- In fact, I'm gonna suggest that the more we can give, while enjoying the process, the more we're going to love our lives."
- Source: Tiny Buddha By Jacob Sokol https://tinybuddha.com/blog/what-you-need-to-live-a-life-of-purpose

FINDING YOURSELF

Your Values + Strengths + Passions + Service = Your Purpose

- "Here's where it all comes together.
- In Scott's post, he wrote, "The intersection of your true values and super powers, backed with relentless passion, is where the magic happens."
- Well I believe, when you find where those things intersect, and then use that for service to others, you'll find the answers to the two big questions, and consequently, know your purpose.
- The equation looks like this:
- Your Values + Strengths + Passions + Service = Your Purpose
- Don't let all the different variables discourage you. Once you dedicate some time for introspection and reflection of those variables, you'll rapidly start to realize the direction you need to move in.
- Start by creating 3 lists:
- Your values
- Your strengths
- Your passions
- The key is to figure out how you can combine your passions and strengths in service to a cause, person, community, or organization other than yourself. Do that and your values will fall into place."
- Source: Tiny Buddha By Jacob Sokol https://tinybuddha.com/blog/what-you-need-to-live-a-life-of-purpose/

THE ACTUAL, PRACTICAL PART OF LIVING ON PURPOSE

- "In her groundbreaking book, The How of Happiness, Positive psychologist Sonja Lyubomirsky wrote that only 10% of happiness comes from extrinsic incentives like money, fame, and status.
- If that's the case, would you be willing to sacrifice some of the money you're making in order to do passionate work that's more fulfilling?
- If so, here's the magic financial formula that you'll need to know:
- Your income must be greater than your expenses!
- That's it—the whole secret. If you're able to start chopping away at your expenses by eliminating non-essential items (like your car, cable TV, eating out, and frivolous shopping), then you'll create an absurd amount of choices and opportunities in your life.
- I know it sounds like a massive lifestyle change to get rid of these things, but a massive lifestyle change may be exactly what you need in order to find and live your purpose.
- We've only got one life to live—and none of us will live forever.
- Don't think that you're being heroic by "toughing it out" and doing things that don't fulfill you. As Frankl wrote, suffering when not necessary is masochistic, not heroic!
- This journey called life will be over before you realize it. Why spend another second living a life that isn't personally meaningful to you?"
- Source: Tiny Buddha By Jacob Sokol https://tinybuddha.com/blog/what-you-need-to-live-a-life-of-purpose/

WHAT ARE THE 7 PRINCIPLES?

- 1. Spend your life discovering your authentic self, then live it to the max – Self-discovery, honesty, and your own truth will set you FREE! Stand up and defend your core values always!

- 2. Do what you love and are good at, and make sure it provides you with real meaning that best matches your purpose. If you discover you're a born leader, don't spend your time alone writing poetry. Or, if you're a talented artist, don't spend your life becoming the next Corporate 100 CEO or President of the U.S.

- 3. Live your world and career in the "We" and become part of something greater than yourself and help others with achieving their success

- 4. Pursue happiness, life-balance, and peace-of-mind/well being alongside your pursuit of success, but never afterwards or you will lose it

- 5. Define your life as a success journey that starts but never ends – forget about the destination, but focus on mastering the process of being successful for you

- 6. Consider humanity, gratitude, self-love, honesty, humility, and charity to be an integral part of any success you seek

- 7. Take complete responsibility for your life, no that failure is a huge part of learning and success, and master resilience in overcoming obstacles

STOP LIVING IN A CONDITIONAL, CONTINGENT WORLD OF "IF-THEN..."

- According to Shawn Achor, Harvard Happiness Expert, we think, "If I can just find that great job, or win that next promotion, lose those ten pounds, or (fill in the blank), then happiness will follow." But Shawn's extensive research and other recent discoveries in the field of positive psychology have shown that this formula is completely backward: Happiness fuels success, not the other way around. When we are positive, our brains become more engaged, creative, motivated, energetic, resilient, and productive at work.

- This isn't just an empty mantra. This discovery has been borne out repeatedly by rigorous research in psychology and neuroscience, management studies, and the bottom lines of organizations around the world. Shawn now spends his time teaching, advising and lecturing at top organizations on how we can — in five easy steps — reprogram our brains to become more positive in order to gain a competitive edge at work and create more success, happiness and reward in our lives.

HOW TO BE HAPPY?

What is Happiness? According to Shawn Achor, Happiness is NOT the belief that everything is great, happiness is the belief that change is possible. In Before Happiness I define happiness as "the joy one feels striving for one's potential." Small mental victories, especially in a rough economy, led us to a cascade of success based on positive changes. What specifically impacts our happiness and how can we shift it? The three greatest predictors of happiness are optimism (the belief your behavior will eventually matter), social connection, and how we perceive stress (as a challenge or as a threat). If we want to raise happiness we need to make both mindset and behavior shifts.

What are the five key steps that we can take each day to increase our experience of happiness?

1. Bring gratitude to mind: Write down three NEW things that you are grateful for each day
2. Journal: About a positive experience you've had recently for two minutes once a day
3. Exercise: Engage in 15 minutes of mindful cardio activity
4. Meditate: Watch your breath go in and out for two minutes a day and
5. Engage in a random, conscious act of kindness: Write a two-minute positive email thanking a friend or colleague, or compliment someone you admire on social media

Do these steps for 21 days, and you will begin to see a lasting shift in your mindset towards more positivity.

WHAT DOES IT MEAN TO BE CHARITABLE & HELP OTHERS?

 It means that you are living out of your head, and your heart and head are humble and other oriented.

 It means that you think about the welfare and contribution to others as a part of your everyday actions

 Being charitable means giving and not just getting. Living in the "We," not just the "I" or "Me."

 What is the best kind of charity? Teaching others how to fish, and not just giving them a fish – and doing so anonymously

 You will find a big part of your meaning and purpose by getting out of self and helping others – always do for others as you would like others to do for you!

HOW DO YOU ACCELERATE YOUR SUCCESS?

- By following the 7 Principles as defined earlier, living your life authentically, with purpose and meaning, and becoming "other" oriented, and leaving the earth a better place than how you found it.
- Live in the here and now, and stop regretting the past and worrying about the future. You're success is right in front of you – in the here and now – Master presence in all your affairs!
- Your success is guaranteed if you have lived your life on purpose, with meaning, and with integrity and authenticity.
- To your life ONE WONDERFUL DAY AT A TIME with NO REGRETS!

KEY TAKE-AWAYS FROM THIS COURSE

- It is time to trash the myth that success is power, money, and prestige
- You need to carefully redefine what success means to you
- It should consider higher values like understanding your purpose and finding meaning in what you end up doing AND how you do it
- Think of success as a process. A life well-lived that include the 7 essential principles for success will always be successful
- Remember that healing your past, and no longer fearing the future will allow you to create a powerful, successful, and meaningful life in the Now – or present moment
- Learn from other successful people, but make sure to adapt their definition to your own and stick to it. Remember that you are on your own journey, take full responsibility for it, own it, and master it!

NEXT STEPS ON YOUR HEALING JOURNEY

- THE HEALING ACADEMY (url/facebook group)
- Healing from Toxic Parents
- Happiness Mastery System
- 21-Day Happiness Challenge
- Making Love Work
- Making Life Work
- Spiritual Journey
- Mindfulness & Meditation
- All my e-books

www.ingramcontent.com/pod-product-compliance
Lightning Source LLC
Chambersburg PA
CBHW051928210526
45473CB00006B/2178